Cloud Engineering for Beginners

Cloud Engineering for Beginners

By Nenne Adaora Nwodo

'Cloud Engineering for Beginners'

www.adoranwodo.com

ISBN: 978-978-996-662-2 (Paperback)
ISBN: 978-978-996-663-9 (Hardcover)
ISBN: 978-978-996-664-6 (Ebook)

Cover and Internal Book Design by Tope Akintola

First published in 2021 by:
Etchwise Consulting Limited
32 Abeokuta Street,
Off Freeman Street,
Ebute-Metta,
Lagos State,
Nigeria

Tel: +234 803 805 9815
www.etchwiseonline.com

10 9 8 7 6 5 4 3 2 1

Table of Contents

Acknowledgments

Writing this book was not a one-person journey. There are multiple people that have inspired me, contributed and supported me throughout this journey.

Firstly, my eternal gratitude goes to God for his grace over my life and his blessings in my career.

Thanks to Angie Jones, a principal engineer who I look up to. Thank you for being an early reader and a contributor to my book. I truly love the foreword you wrote for this book.

Thanks to Hoop Somuah, my engineering manager, who was an early reader and a contributor to my book. Thank you for your feedback and also for helping me put some things in perspective. Thanks for also writing a foreword, I appreciate it.

Thanks to Obinna Nwodo for all the publishing advice and general support.

Thanks to Scott Hanselman who is someone I look up to on so many levels. Thank you for your contribution and agreeing to be a part of his project. I wouldn't trade it for anything.

Thanks to Vaibhav Gujral, a cloud architect I got introduced to when I started writing this book. Thank you for offering to review this book, I learned a lot more about the cloud during this process.

I'm grateful to all my family and friends for their words of encouragement throughout the journey of writing this book, especially on the days when I didn't think I could write anything. Thank you.

It's impossible to list everyone that supported or encouraged me throughout this journey. The little you think you did, made this possible and I appreciate you all for it. Without you, I wouldn't have been able to do this all by myself.

Foreword

By Angie Jones

Tech is hard and ever-changing. Concepts such as "the cloud" seem abstract and difficult to define for beginners and experienced technologists alike. Adora has done the industry a wonderful service by explaining cloud computing in its simplest terms. When Adora told me she'd written this book, I thought "of course she has!". She's just that type of person - one who learns, masters, and then shares her newfound knowledge with the greater engineering community so that we all advance to her level.

"Cloud Engineering for Beginners" is a must-have handbook rich with all you need to know about engineering in the cloud, complete with easy-to-understand definitions, various types of cloud computing and their usages, and viable career paths in cloud engineering.

What I love most about Adora's approach to writing this book is that it is fresh and transparent.

She is honest about concepts that she found confusing as someone new to the industry, discusses her misunderstandings, and uses this opportunity to debunk misunderstandings and heighten the reader's knowledge on the topic.

As a principal-level engineer, I found this book refreshing and enlightening. I wish I had it earlier, as it would have helped me understand these concepts much sooner. I'm grateful to add it to my bookshelf and have no doubt I'll reference it often.

Angie Jones
VP of Global Developer Relations, Block

Foreword

By Hoop Somuah

"The Cloud" has become a central part of the world's technology infrastructure. It's ubiquity increases access to the power of compute, large scale data processing and AI empowering us to transform the way we live, work, play and learn.

I first met Adora near the beginning of her journey in cloud development. In a short while since then, she has become someone I turn to for questions about the latest developments in our own cloud infrastructure. I'm excited that she has chosen to create this introduction for beginners interested in this space and I look forward to seeing more people on their journey to becoming experienced cloud engineers.

Hoop Somuah
Partner Software Engineering Manager, Microsoft Mesh

Foreword

By Scott Hanselman

Is “The Cloud” just a codename for other people’s computers? Yes and no. As with all things in technology, it’s complex. Fortunately Adora breaks it down in this easily digestible book that serves as a great starting point for you if you’re interested in cloud computing. We are all standing on the shoulders of giants as we forge forward towards a cloud-filled future. Complex scaling programs have been solved and been hidden behind a single checkbox or slider bar. But how did we get here?

Adora takes a historical approach and explains how we got here and where we are headed. Once you have understood the concepts introduced here, you’ll feel more comfortable to explore deeper texts and hopefully get cloud certified!

Scott Hanselman
Partner Program Manager, Microsoft
Hanselman.com

Preface

In August 2019, I took on a new role which required me to build cloud services. I had just gotten my bachelors degree a year before and I did not have enough years of work experience under my belt.

Prior to this role, I had experience building web and mobile applications, so programming wasn't entirely a new concept to me. However, in my first few months at my new role, I struggled to understand the reason behind a lot of the tasks I was given. I was able to do them, but a lot of things seemed strange to me.

As time passed, I began to search for answers to a lot of my questions and made a promise to myself to write a book for beginners like me when I got those answers.

Two years later, I am still working on the cloud and I have learned a lot from my co-workers, books and interactions with other engineers on social media and it has brought me here.

This book is about cloud engineering for people without prior experience in cloud technologies or tech in general. To understand why some of these cloud engineering roles exist, we need to understand the concept of the cloud. The goal of this book is to introduce you to cloud computing and then, the different careers paths for cloud engineering.

If you are trying to start a career focused on cloud engineering, this book is definitely for you.

CHAPTER 1

BRIEF HISTORY OF COMPUTING AND THE INTERNET

To be more appreciative of today's technology, we should understand what came before it.

Technology has changed over the years and has also changed the world over the years. The computers that we use today did not exist in the early 1900s. Now, we experience technology on desktop computers, laptops, mobile phones, virtual reality headsets and so much more. To appreciate where we are now, we should think about where it all started from.

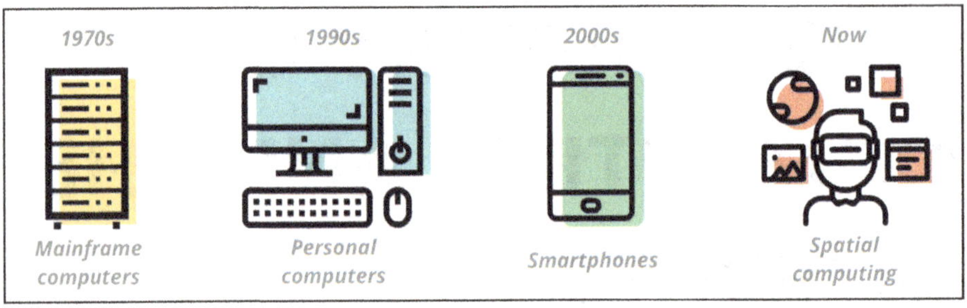

Figure 1.1: The evolution of computing

The evolution of computers

It all began in the 19th century with Charles Babbage, an English mechanical engineer who is considered to be the "father of the computer".

He designed the first general mechanical computer called the Analytical Engine. This computer consisted of an Arithmetic Logic Unit (ALU), basic flow control and integrated memory.

The evolution of computers can be classified into five distinct generations:

- **First generation** - These computers used vacuum tubes as the main components for the processing unit and memory. These vacuum tubes emitted a lot of heat and were very expensive. As a result, these computers weren't accessible and only large organizations were able to afford them. This era was approximately around the 1940s and 1950s.

- **Second generation** - These computers were an improvement on the first generation. In this generation, they were smaller and used cheaper transistors in place of vacuum tubes. Assembly language and other programming languages like FORTRAN were extensively used in this generation. Regardless of the improvements made with respect to size and speed, these computers were still expensive.

- **Third generation** - This generation replaced transistors with integrated circuits. As a result, the computers were a lot smaller and reliable. Here, programming languages like BASIC, PASCAL and FORTRAN II started gaining traction.

- **Fourth generation** - These computers used very large scale integrated (VLSI) circuits. The improvements here gave rise to more powerful, reliable and also affordable computers.

This initiated the personal computer (PC) revolution and up till today, a lot of people still have personal computers in their homes.

- **Fifth generation** - This generation is based on artificial intelligence and parallel processing hardware. We are currently in this era of computing where we are exposed to Robotics, Mixed Reality, Gaming, Internet of things and so on. Today's programmers are now also using evolved programming languages such as Python, JavaScript, C#, C++ and more.

It took a while to get to this point from where we started. We have had new and incredible innovations. Improvements on older inventions (and innovations) have been made too. As computers were improved upon, government researchers were creating ways of sharing information among themselves in the 1960s. This brought about what we know as the internet today.

Introduction to the internet

The internet that we know today was created on January 1st, 1983. The main reason was for sharing information. In the 1960s, computers were large and couldn't be moved around. The only ways to share resources across computers were to personally visit the site with a computer or send magnetic tapes through the postal system.

The cold war also played a role in the creation of the internet. The ARPANET (Advanced Research Projects Agency Network) was created, and it has now evolved into what we call the Internet today.

Introduction to the world wide web

The world wide web is not the same thing as the internet and was created by Sir Tim Berners-Lee, a British computer scientist in 1989.

The web gives everyone access to different documents that exist on the internet. As HyperText Transfer Protocol (HTTP) was created as a standard for communication between different user's computers and servers, companies like Netscape and Microsoft started creating browsers that made going through websites easy.

Today, we create and share content on our websites, social media or other locations on the internet. We are able to do this because of the existence of the world wide web (www).

In the next chapter, we'll get introduced to cloud computing, which is a form of computing that exists because we have the internet today

CHAPTER 2

CLOUD COMPUTING

Is the cloud just someone else's computer? Let's find out in this chapter.

People say cloud computing is offering computing services on the cloud when they want to give a basic definition of the concept. As true as that is, if the concept of the cloud isn't clear, then the definition isn't clear.

Introduction to the cloud

Let's imagine you're logged in to Twitter, Instagram or Facebook on your mobile phone. If you get a new phone and you login, all your direct messages, pictures, videos, tweets and other content still exists as if you never switched phones giving you the same experience across devices. This is possible because we have the cloud. We can use the same application on multiple devices and have the same experience across all devices because most of the computing and storage takes place on the "cloud".

The "cloud" is a set of servers that can be accessed over the Internet. Cloud servers are located in data centers all over the world. These servers exist to store and manage data, run applications or do heavy computing. As opposed to accessing data locally, you can access your data online from any device that can connect to the internet.

An interesting thing about the cloud is that it primarily works on a "pay as you go" model. What this means is that you pay for what you want for as long as you're interested without a lifelong commitment to a provider or plan. Renting cloud computing resources is similar to renting an apartment instead of buying a house. You pay rent for a particular duration and on expiration, you can choose to renew your rent, move to a bigger apartment in the same building or move to a different building.

The cloud is also built on the technologies that enable users to manage and configure resources:

- **Portals:** Management portals exist to make it easy for administrators to manage resources for the applications that run on the cloud.

- **Virtualization:** Virtualization creates a layer of abstraction over hardware with software programs. This allows the hardware components of a computer's CPU, memory, storage etc. — to be partitioned into numerous virtual computers which can be referred to as virtual machines (VMs). This promotes the maximization of hardware on the cloud as multiple users are able to use multiple partitions.

- **Automation:** This helps reduce (or eradicate) manual intervention for tasks such as server provisioning and integration.

Introduction to cloud computing

Now that the concept of the cloud is clearer, we can say that cloud computing is the on-demand availability of computing services on the cloud. This helps businesses worry less about the logistics required in maintaining physical servers so that they can focus on their core business operations. Apart from this, moving all computing to the cloud comes with more benefits:

- **Reliability:** Data and other important resources on the cloud are backed up and can be recovered by the cloud providers if an incident occurs.

- **Scaling:** With the cloud, it's easier to scale up or scale out depending on your business requirements without directly thinking about the background work needed to make that possible.

- **Continuous Delivery:** Your team can set up automatic deployment pipelines so that each small code change makes it to the different environments and regions your applications exist in without manually building and deploying the updated application.

- **Remote friendly:** To access and contribute to cloud applications, all a member of a software engineering team needs is a stable internet connection. Long term, this helps people working in geographically distributed engineering teams collaborate better.

The impact of cloud computing on the startup ecosystem

In very recent times, we've all witnessed the inception and progression of new technology businesses and I believe the cloud has played a very important role in that. Because of the cloud, founders are able to think through their initial product idea, build that product and grow their customer base without worrying about purchasing IT infrastructure or hiring the people to manage and support physical servers (at least in the early stages).

As much as there are a lot of benefits for moving to the cloud, the switch comes with its own set of possible issues. Some of them are listed below:

- **Security Threats:** A public cloud application is accessible to anyone on the internet. This means that when proper security measures aren't taken, there is a probability that hijackers can gain access to your users' data.

On the cloud, the responsibility of enforcing security is on both parties. Cloud providers have to put in the work to make sure that their cloud computing resources are secure. However, no matter how secure these resources are, if the applications deployed by the developers to the cloud aren't security compliant, there is still a huge security risk.

- **Cost on large infrastructure:** Depending on the size of your application infrastructure and the plan for resources like VMs and databases, you could spend a lot of money on cloud infrastructure.

- **Dependency on the service provider:** This isn't always an issue however, if the service provider has downtime or is experiencing performance issues, any cloud application using that provider might experience some issues too. Imagine a scenario where the cloud authentication and authorization platform your application uses is down: during this period, your users would be unable to login to your own application.

Cloud service availability metric

It can be very useful for us to think about the cloud the same way we think about resources or services that we use everyday in our lives.

The most common example is WiFi. When we pay internet bills, we are able to go online and do what we like. However, on some days, we notice that the network reception isn't the best or that there could be short outages. This is because the internet service providers don't have a 100% uptime.

This same way, cloud services have a metric used to measure availability and it is called nines. A low level service may provide an uptime of **two nines** (which is 99%) and a high level service may provide an uptime of **four nines** (which is 99.99%). What this simply means is that for the high level service, 99.99% of the time, you are guaranteed to have a stable service but there's a 0.01% probability of downtime.

The goal for a lot of cloud providers is five nines (99.999% uptime) and even that still has some downtime.

Referring to the previous section on cloud disadvantages, a dependency on a low level cloud service provider means a higher chance of downtime compared to other existing applications on the market.

It is advisable to build resilient applications on resilient cloud providers to reduce the number of outages faced by your users monthly.

Types of cloud computing

There are different variations of the cloud and there is no one-size-fits-all type of cloud computing solution. To determine the kind of solution you need, it's important to understand your business requirements so that you can figure out the best way to run and deploy your applications to the cloud. There are five ways to deploy cloud applications:

- Public cloud
- Private cloud
- Hybrid cloud
- Federal cloud
- Multicloud

The next five subsections cover each cloud computing type.

Public Cloud

As the name implies, a public cloud computing model is for everyone. It allows a third party cloud service provider to make computing resources available to anyone over the internet. These resources can be databases, CPU, storage, virtual machines and more. The computing resources could be available for free or billed on a subscription or pay-as-you-go basis. The pricing would usually depend on the service provider and the type of resource. Examples of public cloud providers are:

Amazon web services (AWS), Google cloud platform (GCP), IBM Cloud, Microsoft Azure and Oracle Cloud.

Since the public cloud is available to everyone, a multi-tenant model is usually adopted to make it possible for the server resources to be shared by multiple customers.

What is Multitenancy

Multitenancy is a software architecture where multiple tenants share a single instance of a software application including data, resources, configuration, and other properties. A tenant is a group of users with the same kind of access and privileges within an application instance. A common way to describe tenants is by using organizations. As an employee working in an organization where your company uses the cloud, you and your co-workers have access to a portal and can see the same resources (with the right permissions made available) because you all exist in the same tenant.

Adopting the public cloud provides room for scalability and flexibility easily in your application because when your application is reporting high latency that is caused by a traffic surge, you can automatically scale up or scale out your processing units. This also exists in databases. If you are running out of database capacity in your current plan, you can always pay for an upgrade only when you need it.

What this means is, with this model, you only get to pay for resources that you actually need which is quite different from private clouds.

Private Cloud

With the private cloud, the servers and computing resources are exclusively assigned to one customer only. This means that, unlike the public cloud, only the customer has access to the software instances on the server.

Unlike the public cloud, the private cloud uses a single-tenant model. This means that the server infrastructure and computing resources are isolated for one particular customer. For this reason, the private cloud is a more secure option for organizations dealing with medical records, financial data or other sensitive information.

The private cloud can be hosted in the organization's private data center or an independent infrastructure from a cloud provider.

Hybrid Cloud

If you were thinking that a hybrid cloud is a combination of the public and private cloud computing models, then you are correct.

The hybrid cloud gives room for more flexibility, more deployment options and better security because it uses technology to combine the super powers of both cloud environments into a single infrastructure for handling all the applications workloads.

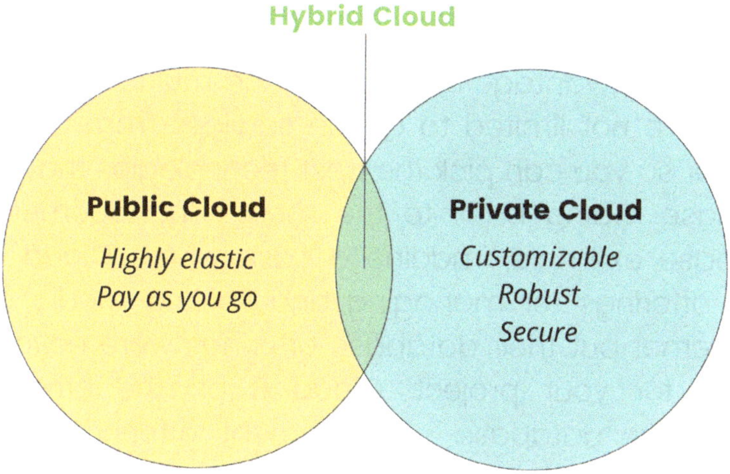

Figure 2.1: Hybrid Cloud Model

Federal Cloud

The federal cloud is bringing the adoption of the cloud to government agencies. The goal is to further enforce cybersecurity and improve the services used by citizens while leveraging the cost-efficient cloud solutions that help support the mission of government agencies.

Multicloud

The multicloud approach means using services from two or more different cloud providers in your cloud application. A typical example of this is using a cloud solution from one provider for managing media in your application while your database is powered by another cloud provider.

A very big advantage of adopting the multicloud model is that you're not limited to all the services from one cloud provider so you can pick the best technologies that fit your use case. Going back to the media management and database example, imagine a case where **Cloud A** has good offerings for managing and serving media across the internet but their database offerings were beyond the budget for your project. **Cloud B** on the other hand provided a database management offering that was affordable but they don't have media management as something they do. With the multicloud model, you can connect to **Cloud A** for their media management solution while running on and leveraging other services from **Cloud B**.

Although the multicloud has this advantage mentioned above, realistically, the more cloud providers used simultaneously, the harder it becomes to manage your applications environment. This happens because each provider has different processes, configurations and tools for their infrastructure management. This can be a disadvantage because, eventually, increased management overhead returns in increased costs. This means using multicloud requires a balance.

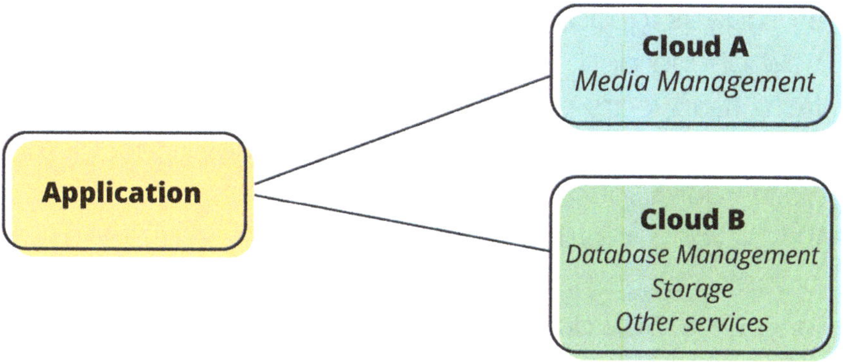

Figure 2.2: Diagram illustrating the Multicloud model

Uses of cloud computing

There are multiple scenarios where cloud computing can be useful to software developers, organizations and the everyday consumer. More often than we realize, we make use of cloud computing indirectly or directly either through the applications we use or because of the fact that we are software developers building the next generation of exciting technology. Here are some domains that use cloud computing today:

- **Continuous deployments and testing:** Cloud computing offers different solutions that help software engineering teams deploy, test and rollback code faster and more efficiently.

- **File storage:** Saving your pictures on your phone's local storage is good, but what happens when you get a new phone and you want to post a throwback picture from four years prior? Do you go through your external drive for the pictures, or do you retrieve the pictures from your iCloud or Google Photos?
  It's beyond pictures. The cloud is an easy and safe place to store documents that you want to have for a long time. You don't need extra space in your purse for an external drive, and you don't need to carry three phones around. All you need is a connection to the internet.

- **Streaming services:** It's possible to watch videos and listen to audio from different geographical locations and across multiple devices on platforms like YouTube, Netflix, Spotify and more because of their cloud computing adoption.

- **On-demand software:** Microsoft Office 365 is an example of this type of software. The cloud makes it possible for application users to access and collaborate on different documents across multiple devices and locations without affecting their overall experience.

We have seen some uses of the cloud for different types of people that exist in the world. It's easy to use streaming services and on-demand software and have shared experiences across devices because they leverage a cloud service model and in the next chapter, we would be going through all the cloud service models.

CHAPTER 3

CLOUD SERVICE MODELS

Depending on your unique business requirement, here are multiple models that exist for cloud computing.

In technology today, an important decision to be made in your business' cloud strategy is choosing the right cloud service model for your business needs. Each model provides customers with different levels of management, versatility and control. Now that we've been introduced to the internet and the concept of cloud computing, we would go through the three main cloud service models that exist on the cloud.

Infrastructure as a Service (IaaS)

With Infrastructure as a Service (IaaS), you're able to rent IT infrastructure from a cloud provider and pay for what you use. Examples of popular cloud infrastructure include: storage, virtual machines and operating systems. This is a good method for reducing cost and transferring logistic risks because the team will not be purchasing and maintaining physical infrastructure. This model gives software engineering teams more flexibility to manage their entire cloud infrastructure themselves.

Advantages of IaaS

- Dynamic scaling: Since IaaS gives on demand self service, teams can scale up and acquire more infrastructure when the need arises. They can also scale down and remove infrastructure when they need to. With the right processes, a team will only be investing in infrastructure that they need at every given time.

- **Cost:** Software engineering teams are able to conserve cost because they do not need to buy more than their required capacity. For example, if the company's business is smaller, they do not have to buy the same amount of capacity as what a much larger company would.

- **Reliability:** System traffic in an IaaS cloud will typically be shared across the different existing servers. If a server is offline, the traffic is routed to another available server. This ensures that there is continuous access to computing resources.

Disadvantages of IaaS

- **Security breach:** Although IaaS providers are responsible for their infrastructures security, software engineering teams need to be responsible for securing their cloud applications. Since the team isn't responsible for the infrastructure security, any breach there introduces a vulnerability that can affect your customers' data.

- **Dependency on the service provider:** The compute resources and data centers belong to the cloud provider. This means that using the IaaS cloud provider creates a dependency on them, which might not be useful in some instances.

Platform as a Service (PaaS)

This model is an extension of the IaaS model. With platform as a service, the cloud provider also provides all the tools for supporting the full lifecycle of a cloud application. PaaS cloud providers take away the need for software engineering teams to manage infrastructure so that they can focus on deploying and managing their applications. This promotes developer efficiency because you focus on your application as opposed to resource procurement and maintenance.

Advantages of PaaS

- Completeness: With PaaS, the software engineering team has a complete platform with tools to build, test and deploy their applications in the same environment.

- Collaboration: Since PaaS cloud gives developers a full suite to build and manage their applications, collaboration is often easier across distributed teams.

- Productivity: With this cloud model, software developers are able to focus only on building, testing and deploying their applications.

Disadvantages of PaaS

- Dependency on the service provider: Like IaaS, the compute resources and data centers in PaaS belong to the cloud provider. This means that using the PaaS cloud provider creates a dependency on them, which might not be useful in some instances.

- Security breach: Customer data exists on the cloud and these things can be confidential. As a result, it is the responsibility of the software engineering teams to implement measures for data safety. This also includes choosing a provider that can guarantee security.

Software as a Service (SaaS)

With software as a service, the cloud provider runs and manages the entire stack. SaaS can be run in a multi-tenant architecture.

With SaaS the team doesn't have to think about the internal workings of the service or infrastructure; all that's important is how to use the service you need.

A common example of a SaaS application is a cloud-based media management service where you can store media for your web applications without thinking about the infrastructure needed to store all the data.

Advantages of SaaS

- Cost: With SaaS, customers can gain access to services through a subscription model that they can cancel anytime.
- Freedom: Customers do not have to manage the software. The responsibility solely belongs to the cloud provider.
- Access: With internet connection, a customer can gain access to SaaS solutions. Due to the fact that everything exists on the cloud, all users will have the same experience and share data using a service across multiple client devices once connection to the internet is established.

Disadvantages of SaaS

- Confidentiality: Organizations storing data in a Saas model would raise security concerns because developers would need to create a secure solution that prevents attackers or other tenants (customers) from viewing data. Even with this, there are still chances of security breaches that could leak confidential information.

- Internet connectivity: Accessing Saas applications requires stable internet connectivity. Without connection to the internet, it's impossible to use these resources effectively and that would have a negative effect on productivity.

CHAPTER 4

CLOUD ENGINEERING

Let's learn about some careers in cloud computing!

Previous chapters of this book have introduced us to the internet, cloud computing and cloud service models. These concepts are the building blocks for cloud engineering. Without them, this profession would not exist today.

What is Cloud Engineering

Cloud engineering focuses purely on applying engineering principles to cloud services. This means a cloud engineer is responsible for planning, architecture, monitoring and management of cloud applications within an organization.

The Cloud Engineer Career Paths

- Cloud Software Engineer: A cloud software engineer designs, builds, tests, debugs and manages applications that run on the cloud. Many kinds of software engineers exist and they build for other platforms and devices.

  A cloud software engineer is able to apply software engineering principles to the cloud. This means that they should have a background in cloud computing.

- **Cloud Security Engineer:** A cloud security engineer provides and continuously improves security on cloud-based systems. These engineers analyze an existing cloud applications security status and come up with strategies to protect data and reduce cyber attacks.

- **Cloud Support Engineer:** A cloud support engineer helps troubleshoot issues reported by customers using the cloud service. They usually work with the cloud software engineers so that they can better understand the way the service works and know how to debug/support it.

- **DevOps Engineer:** In organizations, DevOps engineers help solve the problem of building secure, durable and rapidly evolving distributed systems at scale. They introduce processes, tools and methodologies that make it easy for teams to develop, test and maintain software.

- **Cloud Architects:** The cloud architect's role is to plan the architecture strategy and determine how to design and implement secure cloud infrastructure at scale.

Choosing your path

Sometimes depending on where you find yourself, you might choose a cloud engineering career path. Other times depending on the type of work you're exposed to and the level you are in your journey, a path might choose you.

Here are some tips for choosing a career path if you find yourself in that category:

- **Review the different paths:** In the previous subsection, there are paths to a cloud engineering career. The first step would be to review each path and find the domains that best fit your skills and personality. When reviewing a path, you could also consider factors like community and availability of resources. These things affect how you learn, especially in the beginning.

- **Learn the fundamentals:** At this point, you would have chosen areas you'd like to focus on and you should start from the beginning - which means learning the fundamentals first.

- **Specialize in a particular technology:** After learning these fundamentals, you would need to apply that knowledge to a particular technology. That way, you can attain a high level of mastery in that technology.

There are multiple factors that could affect the technologies you choose to specialize in. It could be:

- Ease of learning
- Availability of jobs
- How much you enjoy working with that technology etc.

For example, you can choose to follow the cloud software engineer path and specialize in C# and other .NET technologies while someone else who is also a cloud software engineer specializes in Java technologies.

Navigating multiple Cloud Engineering paths

In the previous section, I mentioned that it is possible for a Cloud Engineering path to choose you, depending on where you are in your journey.

Using myself as an example, I am primarily a Cloud Software Engineer. However, I've worked on projects that required me to wear multiple hats and I worked across Software Engineering, Security and DevOps. The truth is, most times, these cloud skills could possibly overlap and you may find yourself working on tasks that make you build experience in multiple paths.

When this happens, your ability to keep an open mind and embrace a growth mindset will help you learn and discover more things about the cloud and possibly open you up to more opportunities.

Don't limit yourself to one path if you are ever in a scenario where this happens. Everything is connected.

Here's an example of how Software Engineering and DevOps are connected to Security which can further validate the point that these roles overlap:

- *The Cloud Software Engineer should learn to optimize for security when writing code that deals with application secrets, authentication etc.*

- *The DevOps Engineer that manages application resources should understand that it is a bad idea for every identity to have over privileged access to production resources. They should also understand that for security reasons, resources like virtual machines and DNS record sets should never be left in a vulnerable state.*

CHAPTER 5

SOFTWARE ENGINEERING ON THE CLOUD

Who is a Cloud Software Engineer and what skills do they need?

In this chapter, I'd share with you more details about software engineering on the cloud and the skills I believe you need to become a cloud software engineer.

A lot of times, I'd call myself a software engineer who builds cloud services, because that's a way for me to explain what I do to anyone asking. However, when having conversations with beginners and people that don't work in technology related fields, this definition isn't enough to help them understand who a cloud software engineer is.

Who is a Cloud Software Engineer?

Currently, I build mixed reality cloud services and when I'm asked about what I do, I tell people that I work to build tools that exist on Azure so that other developers using the Azure cloud for their business can connect their augmented or virtual reality applications to these tools.

What does this mean?

As a cloud software engineer, you will build tools or services for an existing cloud provider so that other software engineers around the world (who want to create amazing things with technology) can add the cloud service you created to their application.

This is beyond backend web development; It's not just about building and hosting an API on the internet, it's about building products and services on the cloud so that other people can build consumer applications.

What skills should a Cloud Software Engineer have?

- Computer science fundamentals: Whenever I'm writing an article or speaking at an event, I always share that learning the fundamentals of computer science are building blocks that you need for any type of software engineering career. These fundamentals expose you to operating systems, networking, databases and so on.

- Programming: A cloud software engineer writes code like other software developers, so programming is an important skill. Depending on what cloud you're building for and the stack you're working with, the programming languages you're required to know may vary.

- Problem solving: In all areas of tech, you're going to solve problems. It could be problems from customers (e.g. handling large traffic), or problems that you created yourself (e.g. bugs). Knowing how to break large problems down into smaller units and solving them one after the other is a very valuable skill.

- Cloud computing: To build for the cloud, it's important to understand the concept of cloud computing and differentiate the models that exist. Knowing about cloud service providers and their offerings also helps solidify your cloud knowledge.

- Soft skills: No matter what field you find yourself in tech, soft skills are of paramount importance. This is because you'd always be building for, and working with people. Being an effective team player wherever you find yourself is an essential skill.
  There are different soft skills that exist, and I cannot possibly list everything here. However, I believe that embracing interdependence, proactivity and teachability will help in your journey.

- Web services & APIs: When trying to transform data or process information, we use the IPO (input-process-output) model. This means that I can give a system some input and that system processes my data and gives me my result (output). When we build cloud services, we will want clients using our service to pass data that we can process and we return an output.

This means we would need to create a way for these systems to exchange data with our service and that's where the knowledge of APIs and web services come in.

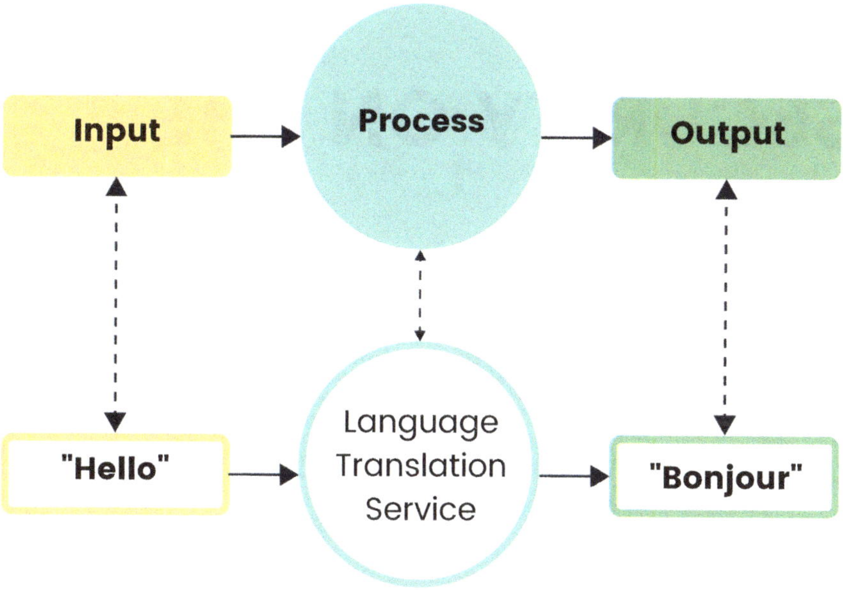

Figure 5.1: Sample Input-Process-Output for a french language translation service

CHAPTER 6

SECURITY ON THE CLOUD

How do we approach security for our cloud applications?

Before learning about cloud security, I assumed that the cloud provider had the sole responsibility of making the cloud cyber-attack free. I was chatting with a friend once and that conversation made me realize that: when building cloud services, there are usually security requirements that must be met before that service is released for general availability.

This means that, for success, the security responsibility is shared between the cloud provider and the organizations building and deploying their cloud applications.

We know the cloud to be a collection of servers that can be accessed over the internet and this means that poor security could make computing resources and customers' data susceptible to digital attacks. Designing processes that improve security on the cloud is for our long-term benefit.

Who is a Cloud Security Engineer?

The role of a cloud security engineer is to provide and continuously improve security for cloud applications. This usually means creating and enforcing methodologies that protect the systems, networks and data from cyberattacks.

Real life scenario

Imagine there was a bucket of water on the corridor of your apartment and that water is supposed to be for you and your housemate alone. You and your housemate go to fetch water when you need it, but somehow, other people outside of the apartment come to take water from that bucket and you're not aware of this until a day that someone pours a dirty substance into the bucket making it unfit for you and your housemate to use.
A good way to ensure that the water was secure would have been to create a lockable tap and only give keys to the apartment residents.

From this real life scenario, we can try to draw parallels with cloud security as well. Let's think of the bucket as a cloud resource: a cloud security engineer would make sure that resources are accessed by authorized users and the application meets all the necessary security requirements.

Cloud Security Focus Areas

- Cloud compliance: Let's consider this, in the finance industry, there are guidelines concerning money deposits and cash transactions. Another case would be the insurance sector that has guidelines on how insurance companies operate and how premiums are calculated.

Similarly, cloud services should be compliant with standards that are useful for their customers. In the context of data protection on the cloud, a common example is the GDPR (General Data Protection Regulation) requirement. This requirement ensures that for operations within the EU member state, certain data protection and privacy principles must be followed.

As a result, the security teams for cloud service providers operating in the EU would have to make sure that their services are GDPR compliant to prevent legal issues.

- **Infrastructure and application security:** In the cloud, providers secure their operating system and physical infrastructure while PaaS (Platform as a Service) customers secure their application and data.

  However, when building a cloud application that will be hosted on this infrastructure, there are some best practices that take you steps closer to meeting your applications security objectives:

  - **Threat Modelling:** This is an engineering process that allows you to identify possible threats, vulnerabilities and attacks in your application. If there are design flaws that attackers can take advantage of, the team would learn about that during this process. Incorporating threat modelling as part of an engineering process allows teams to better enhance security and mitigate identified threats.

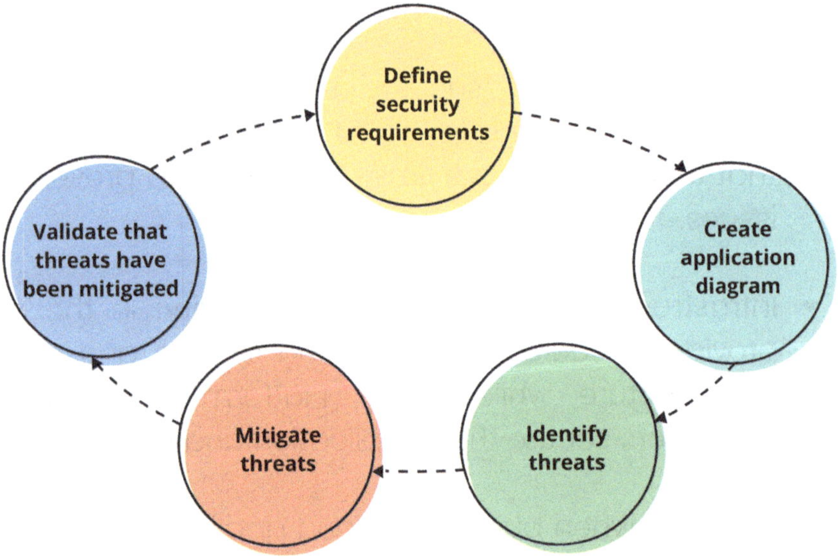

Figure 6.1: Threat modelling steps

- **Validate that there are no inherited security vulnerabilities:** Vulnerabilities in applications or libraries are easy ways for attackers to take advantage of an application. External libraries usually have these security vulnerabilities and doing a regular audit to identify these issues and fix them in time helps reduce potential security threats.

- **Protect application resources:** Each point of interaction is a way for attackers to gain access to an application. Preventing these attacks requires work that limits access of the application to untrusted users.
  Implementing proper identity and access management strategies allows developers to access only the resources and features that they are privileged to use at the required level.

- **Data protection:** When building applications that store and transmit sensitive customer data, a secure data protection strategy is required to prevent attackers from stealing information belonging to multiple users. Encrypting data at rest and using secure data transmission protocols can help improve data protection.

- **Leverage on the cloud providers security features:** Cloud providers offer multiple security features, guidelines and support for building cloud services hosted on their infrastructure, so it's a great place to start.

CHAPTER 7

DEVOPS

"DevOps is deeper than a role, it is a culture"

For a very long time, my idea of the concept of DevOps was very flawed. I used to think that DevOps started and ended with continuous integration and continuous delivery (CI/CD). In reality, CI/CD is just one of the many DevOps practices.

DevOps is deeper than a role. It is a culture.

Before I started working in DevOps, I tried to read about the concept to understand what it meant. Every internet search or book I opened in that time would explain DevOps as:

> *"A set of practices that bridge the gap between software developers (Dev) and IT operations staff (Ops) "*

I have this definition stuck in my head, but for a long time, I didn't fully understand what it meant or why that gap needed a bridge in the first place.

The truth is: to appreciate DevOps, we have to understand what existed before it.

What existed before DevOps

Prior to the introduction of DevOps, most software development teams used the waterfall methodology - a sequential model where each software development process depends on the previous phase.

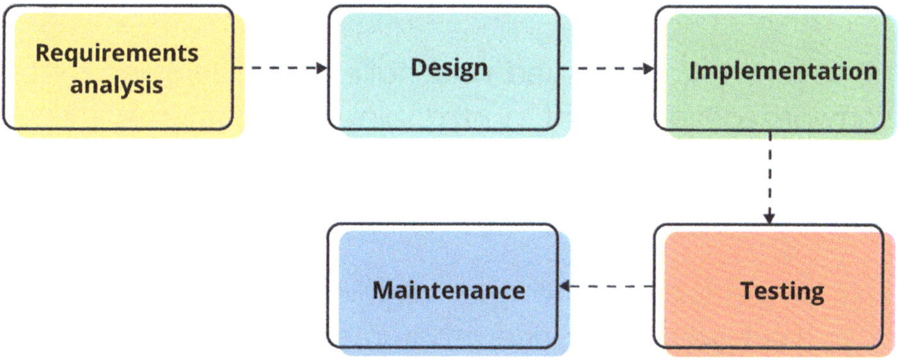

Figure 7.1: The waterfall methodology

In this model, software development teams would spend months building a new feature in an application. After the implementation, they spend more time deploying that new code to the existing application and running tests to be sure everything worked as it should. What this meant was that it took several months to ship a new feature and bugs weren't usually caught on time.

To make the software development process less painful, teams started adopting agile methodologies.

These methodologies were more iterative than sequential and meant that updates were made more frequently in small bits. This new concept had it's advantages:

- Bugs created in small changes can be found a lot faster.
- Smaller code changes can be deployed faster.

However as time passed and agile methodologies made software development and deployment faster, it further exposed other siloed IT roles like testing, security, monitoring and management.

This realization led to the beginning of DevOps; new processes were introduced that integrated CI/CD into the rest of the software delivery lifecycle. This integration between Dev and Ops makes it possible for people to collaborate and produce more secure and reliable applications faster.

The DevOps Lifecycle

- **Planning:** In this phase, teams scope out features of the application they are trying to build. They prioritize tasks and track the progress of each task.

In this phase, a backlog of value adding features and bugs that need to be fixed are created for the team to follow.

- **Development:** This is where the software developers build new features by writing, reviewing and testing their code based on the work items that exist in the backlog.

- **Continuous Integration:** In this phase, the new code is integrated into the existing codebase and tested. After that, an updated artifact or executable is created and ready for deployment.

- **Deployment:** Here, the build output (executable or artifact) from the continuous integration step is deployed to the environments the team uses. Normally, teams have development and staging environments that are different from the production environments their customers use. When the new change is deployed to the non-production environment and errors are detected, they easily rollback changes to prevent buggy features from getting rolled out to customers.

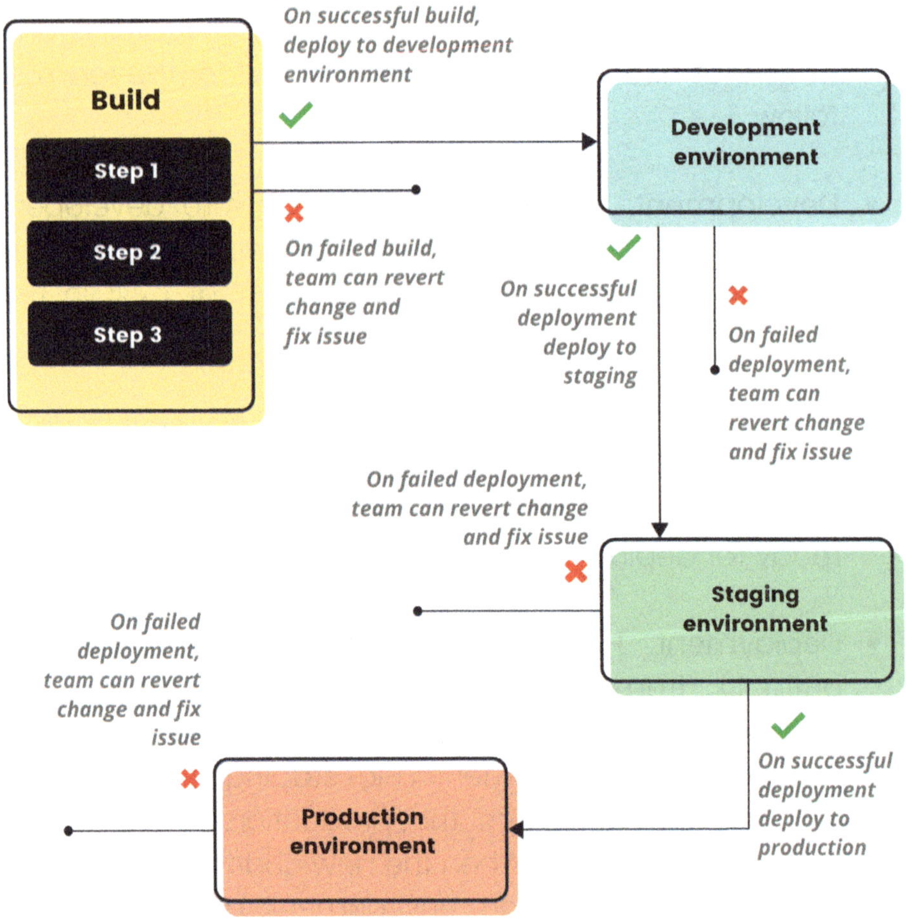

Figure 7.2: Continuous integration and deployment

- **Monitoring:** This phase involves monitoring and maintaining applications in production environments. This phase ensures that the application is running smoothly by constantly checking metrics like performance and availability. If something goes wrong, incidents are created and the appropriate people work on fixing these incidents to restore the application to its desired state.

- **Feedback:** This involves gathering customer feedback on features and overall performance of the application. Sometimes, there could be feature requests. All this information is taken and would be used to plan future releases. The feedback phase is important because it makes software development teams continuously improve on their product.

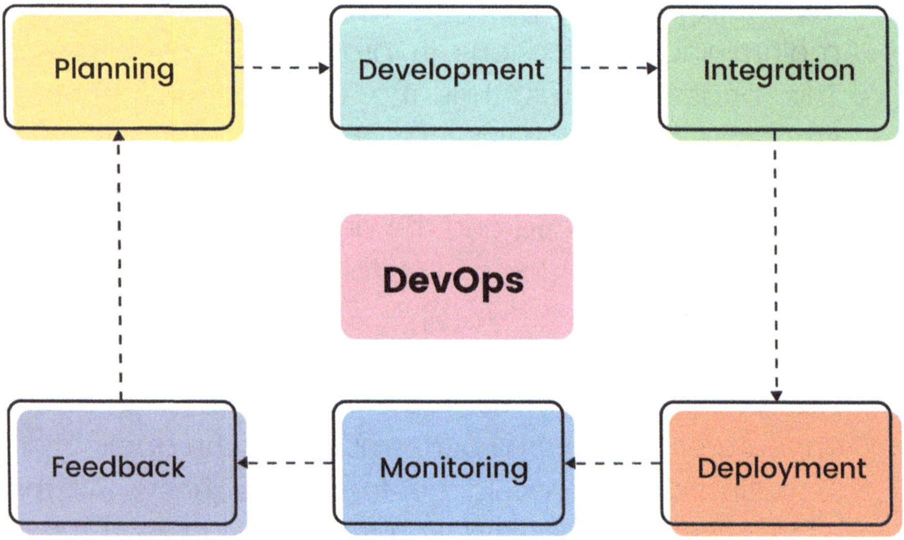

Figure 7.3: The DevOps lifecycle

CHAPTER 8

CLOUD NATIVE APPLICATIONS

Let's learn about the new approach for building and deploying complex applications on the cloud.

As we take our time to explore the evolution of the cloud, one thing is constant and that is innovation.

Due to digital innovation, we find ourselves building more complex systems while delivering to our customers in record time, and with zero downtime. As a result, we have come to adopt a new approach for building and deploying applications called **Cloud Native**. This approach helps us fully exploit the advantages of cloud computing.

Cloud native technologies empower organizations to build and run scalable applications in modern, dynamic environments such as public, private, and hybrid clouds. Containers, microservices, service meshes, immutable infrastructure, and declarative APIs exemplify this approach.

These techniques enable loosely coupled systems that are resilient, manageable, and observable. Combined with robust automation, they allow engineers to make high-impact changes frequently and predictably with minimal toil.

- Cloud Native Computing Foundation

The Cloud Native Computing Foundation

The **Cloud Native Computing Foundation** (CNCF), is an open source software foundation created by the Linux Foundation for exclusively promoting the adoption of Cloud Native technologies.
The CNCF supports communities focusing on Kubernetes, CoreDNS and Prometheus as well as organizations building container orchestration tools within a microservice architecture.

Advantages of Cloud-Native Applications

- Due to the microservice architecture, the components of cloud native applications can be built and deployed independently of each other. This means that a component would not be updated unless it has to be.

- Continuous Delivery (and the DevOps culture in general), helps create an environment where building, deploying and testing applications happen more consistently through automation.

- Container orchestration tools like Kubernetes make it possible to deploy applications without having any downtime. Zero downtime deployments are very good for business as they prevent interruptions in a customer's experience.

These advantages exist as a result of the cloud native building blocks.

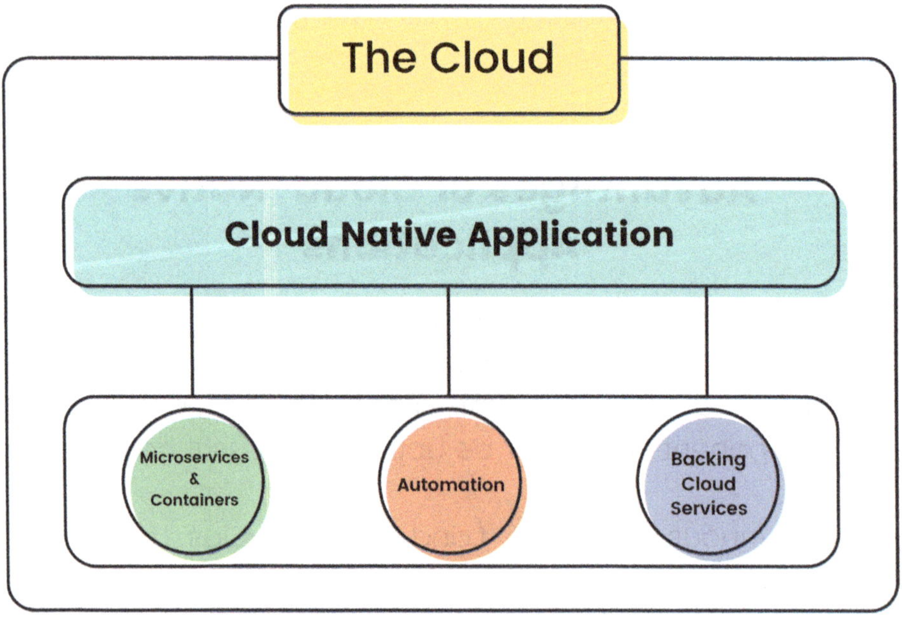

Figure 8.1: Cloud Native building blocks

Microservices

Microservices are an architectural pattern where an application consists of multiple smaller and independently deployable components that interact with each other. Before the microservice architecture was introduced, enterprise applications worked a lot with the monolith architecture.

With monoliths, everything is tightly coupled into one service. Meaning that if a process in the application needs to scale, the entire application must scale. As the application grows, this might become problematic.

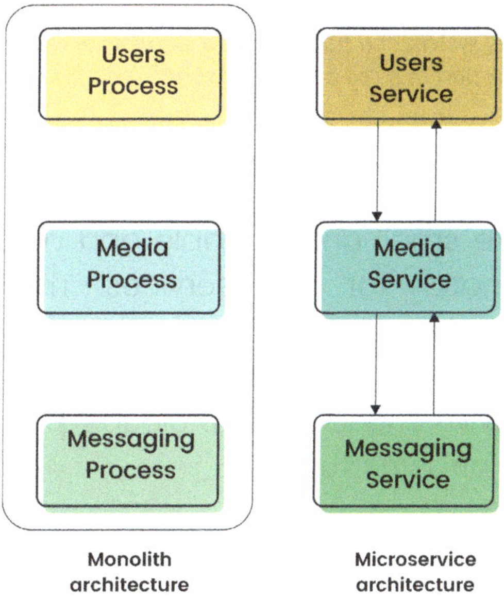

Figure 8.2: Monolith vs Microservice

Containers

With containers, cloud native applications can be abstracted from the environments where they run. They help package source code along with libraries and dependencies so that the code can run anywhere. For this to happen effectively, containers take advantage of virtualization.

What is Virtualization

Virtualization uses technology to create a layer of abstraction over computer hardware. This allows the hardware elements of a single computer (e.g. CPU, memory, storage etc.) to be divided into multiple virtual computers. We call these virtual computers ***virtual machines*** *(VMs). Each virtual machine runs on its own operating system and behaves like a standalone computer, even though it runs on a small part of a computer hardware.*

Containers are small and portable and as a result, are a very good match for microservices. They amplify the benefits of microservices by enabling a consistent deployment and management experience across a hybrid multicloud environment - public clouds, private cloud and on-premises infrastructure.

Backing Cloud services

When building cloud native applications, it's normal for these systems to depend on resources like databases, storing services, caching services and more. The services are already made available and managed by cloud providers and are called backing cloud services. Cloud providers release SDKs and APIs that allow other developers to communicate with these services when building their own cloud native applications.

Automation

To achieve the speed and agility that cloud native brings, a very important piece of that puzzle is automation. Automation happens on two levels:

- Automated deployments: With continuous integration and continuous deployments, teams automate the release of application updates to customers by writing scripts that run on build and release pipelines.

- Infrastructure automation: This involves the ability to deploy cloud resources (e.g. storage services, virtual machines, databases, network infrastructure etc.) using source code and other scripts as opposed to provisioning this infrastructure manually on the portal of the cloud provider. Infrastructure automation thrives on a concept called Infrastructure as Code (IaC).

With Infrastructure as Code, developers can use high-level programming languages to automate the provisioning of infrastructure. A major advantage for IaC is that it helps eliminate configuration drift, which means that no matter how many times the code is run, it would always produce the same set of resources with the same configurations.
Like normal code, infrastructure code can also be versioned, tested and rolled back if the need arises.

CHAPTER 9

GETTING READY FOR A CLOUD ENGINEER INTERVIEW

Some important steps to take when looking out for cloud jobs.

When looking for your next job, your interviews are very critical and determine whether you will receive an offer or not. As a result, being prepared for interviews makes you one step ahead and that gives you the control and confidence needed to show the employers that you are a great cloud engineer.

I've listened to people talk about steps they took when getting ready for job interviews and some things are always common. After watching these tips work for myself and other people that I have interacted with, I now believe that these are important steps that you should take when getting ready for your cloud engineer job interview.

- **Build a portfolio:** When looking for a new tech job, a portfolio helps you stand out to recruiters and hiring managers. Building a portfolio gives you an opportunity to showcase your skills and depth by highlighting the different projects you've worked on, other past contributions and previous experience.

  These would give employers an insight into how you would contribute to their team if they hired you.

  After building your portfolio, it's important to share it within your network: taking advantage of the different communities that exist online can expose you to roles in cloud engineering and beyond. I've seen people get great opportunities from social media because they built a portfolio and became intentional about sharing their work.

1. **Career Summary**
   Highlights career interests and accomplishments
2. **Skills and Certifications**
   Showcases your competence to everyone
3. **Experience**
   Showcases your career history to everyone
4. **Work Projects**
   Showcases the impact you've made at your current and previous jobs
5. **Passion Projects**
   Showcases the impact you've made in your community
6. **Education**
   Share your educational achievements (if applicable)
7. **Volunteering**
   Have you volunteered to speak, mentor or organize events? Add that too!

Figure 9.2: What each section in your portfolio should contain

- **Make direct contact with recruiters:** Some people submit resumes and get job interviews. A lot of people don't. The challenge with applying on job search platforms is that there are millions of great people applying too and it's easy for your application to get lost. However, reaching out to recruiters either via social media or career fairs puts you at the front of these people and gives you the ability to sell yourself directly. This way, when you send in your application, there's a higher probability of getting a call back.

  Another way to be guaranteed an interview is to consistently build a professional online presence and have these recruiters reach directly to you. The beauty is that top companies are always hiring and their recruiters are always scouting for talent. If you're able to position yourself in a way that they would reach out to you directly via social media or your website, you would definitely get a spot to interview.

A short story

Three years before joining Microsoft as a full time employee, I had applied for the Microsoft 4Afrika internship and never got a call back. This doesn't mean that my application was not good, but I was in the pool with so many good people and I got skipped.
Few years later, a recruiter reached out to me for my current role, which meant they had already noticed me and as a result, I got a call back and scheduled interviews.

- **Practice technical questions:** Before the interview day, you should brush up on technical questions. This is a very important part of the preparation process because teams want to hire people that are technically sound and you should strive to make sure your technical depth matches the promise in your application.

  If you're applying for a DevOps role, brush up on DevOps practices, networking, operating systems and things concerning cloud providers. Software engineers should practice systems design as well as data structures.

- **Practice situational questions:** There would always be at least one non-technical interview during that process and preparing for that is also very important. Here, interviewers want to know if you're a good culture fit and most times, they would ask you situational questions to know how you've handled issues or demonstrated soft skills in the past.

- **Do mock interviews:** A mock interview is a practice job interview with a professional or friend in preparation for the actual interview. Putting yourself in these practice scenarios help you build confidence required to answer technical questions and talk about yourself.

In mock interviews, you could make some mistakes and your practice interviewer can let you know what those shortcomings are so that you can learn and improve before going for the real interview.

- Learn about the company you're interviewing with: Personally, I see interviews as a two way thing. As much as I'm being interviewed so that the team knows if I'm a good technical and culture fit, I'm also interviewing them to know if they're a good fit for my goals and I always advise people to do the same.

  As a result, I believe it's important to ask questions during interviews. The answer to those questions will give you an idea about the kind of company you're considering working at. It's easy to know what to ask when you've done prior research about the organization so that you don't ask vague questions and get vague answers.

CHAPTER 10

LONG TERM CAREER GROWTH TIPS

You finally got a job. Here's how to keep growing in your career.

From the beginning of this book till this point, you have been reading about the cloud and the different roles that exist in that space.

At some point in your career, you will want to grow beyond beginner or intermediate. You might be thinking about following the management or individual contributor track as you advance in your career. In this section, I am sharing long term career growth tips that I have picked up from professionals around me:

- **Build a personal brand:** Personal branding positions you as an authority or thought leader in your industry. This means that people know you for the work you do and this, in turn, elevates your credibility as a cloud engineer.

  A personal brand is great because it makes you stand out, increases your network and connects you to multiple people that can help in your career journey.

- **Own your learning:** You own your career and have the power to steer it in whatever direction you want. If you're very keen about your career advancement, make it a habit to learn interesting skills and technologies that get you closer to where you want to be.

Many companies have growth programs and education opportunities for employees. You can take advantage of these training sessions, conferences and learning materials.

Outside your current company, you can also choose to take courses on credible platforms where you can get knowledge about a new technology and certifications (if that's something you're interested in).

- **Reflect on your journey periodically:** Looking back at your last six months (or one year) could be a good way to track your career growth. Constantly do a self evaluation by asking questions like this:
    - What did I do in the last 6 months?
    - What am I doing now?
    - How have I improved in 6 months?
    - What would I want to do in the next 6 months?

- **Have a career mentor:** Most times, this can be your manager. But, I strongly believe that it's important to have someone at a higher level that you can communicate with about your career growth. They can give advice and also expose you to opportunities that get you to where you want to be.

CHAPTER 11

Hello, Cloud!

It's time to do more!

So, that's it. We are at the end of this book and I am very proud of you for making it this far. This chapter is titled "Hello, Cloud!", because, although we have come to the end of this book, this is not the end for you, but the beginning.

It's the beginning of your new journey into a career in cloud engineering. I hope you can put all the information in this book to practice so that you can maximize your potential as you go forward in this career path. I'm excited for you and I hope you do well. I'm rooting for you ❤️

You ought to be all set now; so go forth, learn more, share, and join me in building the next innovative technology on the cloud.

Adora

About the Author

Nenne Adaora Nwodo (who fondly likes to be called Adora), is a Software Engineer. She currently works at Microsoft where she builds cloud services related to Artificial Intelligence and Mixed Reality.

In 2018, she created a blog called AdoraHack where she publishes articles on Software Engineering, Productivity & Career Growth. In June 2019, she created a YouTube channel for AdoraHack where she posts tech content that could be useful to Software Developers. In March 2021, she won the Young CISO Network Excellence in Disruptive Technology, Cloud and Embedded Device Security Award for her work in building and advocating for Disruptive Technology on the Cloud.

Adora is extremely passionate about the developer community and is driving inclusion for women in technology. She co-organizes community events, contributes to open source and speaks at technology conferences worldwide.

Made in the USA
Monee, IL
03 November 2026

67383131R00049